BEING SAFE ON WHEELS

Published by The Child's World®
1980 Lookout Drive • Mankato, MN 56003-1705
800-599-READ • www.childsworld.com

ACKNOWLEDGMENTS
The Child's World®: Mary Berendes, Publishing Director
The Design Lab: Design and production
Red Line Editorial: Editorial direction

LIBRARY OF CONGRESS CATALOGING-IN-PUBLICATION DATA
Kesselring, Susan.
  Being safe on wheels / by Susan Kesselring;
illustrated by Dan McGeehan.
     p. cm.
  Includes bibliographical references and index.
  ISBN 978-1-60954-371-6 (library bound)
  1. Sports—Safety measures—Juvenile literature. 2. Children's
accidents—Prevention—Juvenile literature. 3. Wheels—Juvenile
literature. I. McGeehan, Dan, ill. II. Title.
  GV344.K465 2011
  796.028'9—dc22   2010040480

Printed in the United States of America
Mankato, MN
December, 2010
PA02069

About the Author

Susan Kesselring loves children, books, nature, and her family. She teaches K-1 students in a progressive charter school down a little country lane in Castle Rock, Minnesota. She is the mother of five daughters and lives in Apple Valley, Minnesota, with her husband, Rob, and a crazy springer spaniel named Lois Lane.

About the Illustrator

Dan McGeehan spent his younger years as an actor, author, playwright, and editor. Now he spends his days drawing, and he is much happier.

How do you like to ride? Is **in-line skating** your thing? Do you zoom down the street on your bike? Or do you like riding ramps and doing tricks on your skateboard?

Rolling on wheels is tons of fun. But you can get hurt if you're not careful. That's why you should learn how to be safe on your favorite wheels!

Does your bike fit you? Make sure it does. A **salesperson** can help you pick a bike that is the right size for you.

Check out the bike's seat. It should be tall enough so your knees bend just slightly when the pedals are closest to the ground. Next, look at the handlebars. They should be as high as the seat. Lastly, sit on your bike. Make sure you can place your feet flat on the ground.

Keep your music player off until after you're done wheeling. Headphones can keep you from hearing cars coming your way.

Whatever wheels you ride, be sure to wear the right safety gear. Always wear a helmet. It can save your life if you fall hard.

Your helmet should fit **snug** on your head. The front of the helmet should sit about one inch above your eyebrows. Only one or two fingers should fit between the strap and your chin.

Some kids might think helmets look silly. But nothing's cooler than something that can save your life! In some states, it's the law to wear a helmet.

Next step—pads. On a scooter, wear elbow and knee pads. Add wrist guards for skateboarding and in-line skating. Pads can keep you from breaking bones and getting major cuts if you crash.

When using your bike, skateboard, or scooter, wear shoes that stay on your feet—not flip-flops or slip-ons. You don't want to scrape your toes. Tie those laces tight so they don't get caught in the pedals.

Great! You've got your safety gear on.
Now it's time to check a few things.
Try the brakes on your bike or scooter
to make sure they work. Feel the tires.
They should be full
of air. Check
your wheels
to make sure
they're free of
sticks, rocks, and
other things.
You're ready
to roll!

It's not a good idea to ride your wheels at night. It is hard to see where you are going in the dark. Cars can't see you as well, either.

No matter what kind of wheels you ride, stay on pavement. Avoid dirt, gravel, and potholes. If you hit a bump, you could lose your **balance** and crash. Avoid wheeling through water. It could be slippery.

Most wheels are built for one person to ride. Don't let friends ride your bike, skateboard, or scooter with you.

On a bike and a scooter, it's always best to keep both hands on the handlebars at all times. You might have to quickly steer away from something. It's easier to do this with both hands on the handlebars.

Ride away from the road. Focus on the path in front of you as you ride. If you need to carry anything, put it in a backpack or bike basket. That way your hands are able to steer the bike.

Riding a skateboard is cool, too! Be sure to ask an adult to watch. Try out a skate park. It is a great place to ride!

If you want to learn skateboarding tricks, ask if you can take a skateboarding class. If you can't, that's okay, too. You can learn a trick from another friend or an older sibling. Just make sure an adult is there. You shouldn't try tricks on your own.

The part of the skateboard the rider stands on is called the deck. It's made of wood, plastic, or aluminum. Most decks are about 9 inches (23 cm) wide and 32 inches (81 cm) long.

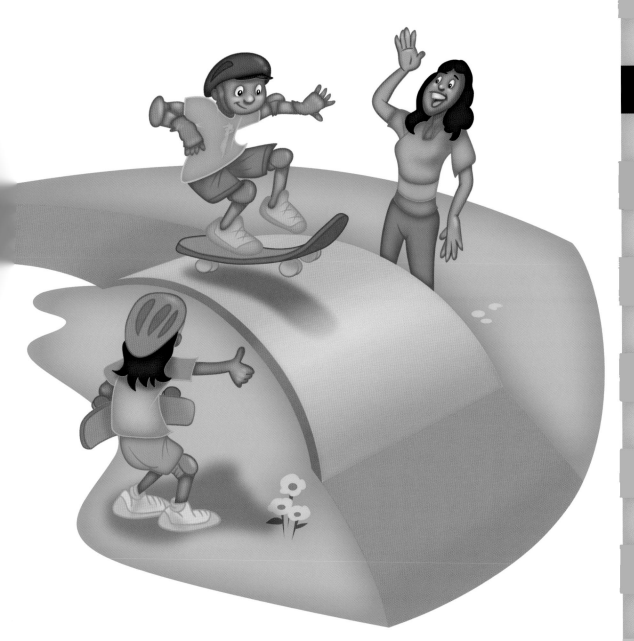

Have you been in-line skating? It is a great way to get around. But you need to know how to stop. Then you won't roll into the street or go so fast you lose control and fall. In-line skates usually have breaks on the back. To use one, tip one foot up so the break rubs on the ground. This will slow you down. Practice using the brake until you're good at stopping. Slow down when you go around a curve, too.

The street is not a safe place to ride. Stay on the sidewalk. Even better, see if an adult will take you to a bike path or a park.

You can go so fast on wheels! Bike around the park, scoot on a bike path, or just skate down the block. However you're rolling, be safe and have fun!

WHEELING SAFETY RULES TO REMEMBER

Always be safe!

1. Always wear a helmet.

2. Wear the necessary pads and guards.

3. Make sure your bike, scooter, or skates fit you.

4. Check your wheels before you use them.

5. Find a smooth, dry place to ride.

6. Pay attention to what is around you when you are on your wheels.

7. Have an adult nearby when learning tricks.

GLOSSARY

balance (BAL-uhnss): Balance is your ability to stay steady and not fall to the ground. Ride your wheels on a clear path to keep your balance.

in-line skating (IN-lyn SKAY-ting): In-line skating is moving on skates that have all the wheels in a straight line. Always wear a helmet when in-line skating.

salesperson (SAYLZ-pur-sun): A salesperson is someone who sells you something. You may buy a bike from a salesperson.

snug (SNUG): If something is snug, it fits not too tightly and not too loosely. Make sure your helmet is snug on your head.

TO LEARN MORE

BOOKS
Llewellyn, Claire. *Watch Out! On the Road*.
Hauppauge, NY: Barron's Educational Series, 2006.

Mattern, Joanne. *Staying Safe on My Bike*. Milwaukee,
WI: Weekly Reader Early Learning Library, 2007.

Pancella, Peggy. *Bicycle Safety*. Chicago:
Heinemann Library, 2005.

WEB SITES
Visit our Web site for links about being safe on wheels:
childsworld.com/links

Note to Parents, Teachers, and Librarians: We routinely
verify our Web links to make sure they are safe and active
sites. So encourage your readers to check them out!